What's in the MIDWEST?

By Robin Johnson

Crabtree Publishing Company

www.crabtreebooks.com

Crabtree Publishing Company

www.crabtreebooks.com

Author: Robin Johnson
Publishing plan research and development:
  Sean Charlebois, Reagan Miller
  Crabtree Publishing Company
Editor: Lynn Peppas
Proofreader: Crystal Sikkens
Editorial director: Kathy Middleton
Photo research: Crystal Sikkens
Designer: Ken Wright
Production coordinator: Ken Wright
Prepress technician: Ken Wright
Print coordinator: Katherine Berti

Photographs:
Peter Newark American Pictures/The Bridgeman
  Art Library International: page 16
Dreamstime: cover (St. Louis), pages 7, 11 (bottom),
  17, 21, 23 (corn)
Digital Vision: title page
Fotolia: page 18
iStockPhoto.com: cover (Mt. Rushmore), pages 11
  (top), 23 (top right), 26, 28
Keystone Press: © Kyndell Harkness/
  Zumapress.com: page 27 (bottom)
Photos.com: pages 13, 24
Wikimedia Commons: MadMaxMarchHare: page 6;
  Greg Henshall: cover (ship), 13
All other images by Shutterstock.com

Illustrations:
Barabara Bedell: page 15 (bottom)
Katherine Berti: pages 14, 15 (top right)
Samara Parent: pages 4–5, 6, 10, 20
Bonna Rouse: page 15 (top left)

Cover description: The Gateway Arch is located in St. Louis on the west bank of the Mississippi River. The Mount Rushmore National Memorial in South Dakota is a sculpture of the heads of four presidents of the United States. The Midwest is known as the country's "breadbasket" due to the abundant harvests of crops such as corn, oats, and wheat. Many factories are built near rivers and lakes so that ships can transport their goods.

Title page description: The Old Courthouse resides next to a beautiful fountain in Keiner Plaza in St. Louis, Missouri. In the distance you can see the Gateway Arch, which celebrates the westward expansion of the United States.

Library and Archives Canada Cataloguing in Publication

Johnson, Robin (Robin R.)
  What's in the Midwest? / Robin Johnson.

(All around the U.S.)
Includes index.
Issued also in electronic formats.
ISBN 978-0-7787-1823-9 (bound).--ISBN 978-0-7787-1829-1 (pbk.)

  1. Middle West--Juvenile literature. I. Title. II. Series: All around the U.S.

F351.J65 2012   j977   C2011-904840-X

Library of Congress Cataloging-in-Publication Data

Johnson, Robin (Robin R.)
  What's in the Midwest? / Robin Johnson.
    p. cm. -- (All around the U.S.)
  Includes index.
  ISBN 978-0-7787-1823-9 (reinforced library binding : alk. paper) -- ISBN 978-0-7787-1829-1 (pbk. : alk. paper) -- ISBN 978-1-4271-8777-2 (electronic pdf) -- ISBN 978-1-4271-9595-1 (electronic html)
  1. Middle West--Juvenile literature. I. Title. II. Series.

  F351.J65 2012
  917.7--dc23

                    2011026690

Crabtree Publishing Company

www.crabtreebooks.com   1-800-387-7650

Printed in Canada/092013/TG20130816

Published in Canada
Crabtree Publishing
616 Welland Ave.
St. Catharines, ON
L2M 5V6

Published in the United States
Crabtree Publishing
PMB 59051
350 Fifth Avenue, 59th Floor
New York, New York 10118

Published in the United Kingdom
Crabtree Publishing
Maritime House
Basin Road North, Hove
BN41 1WR

Published in Australia
Crabtree Publishing
3 Charles Street
Coburg North
VIC 3058

CONTENTS

Words that are defined in the glossary are in **bold** type
the first time they appear in the text.

The United States of America

The United States of America is a big, beautiful country. In fact, it is the third-largest country in the world. The United States is part of North America. It **borders** Canada to the north and Mexico to the south. The Atlantic Ocean is east of the United States. The Pacific Ocean is on the west coast of the country.

FIFTY STATES

The United States is made up of 50 **states**. Most of the states in America are found between Canada and Mexico. Alaska and Hawaii, however, are far away from the other states. Washington is the capital of the United States. It is located in a special part of the country called the District of Columbia.

WHAT ARE REGIONS?

The United States is divided into regions. A region is an area that is similar, or almost the same, in important ways. There are many types and sizes of regions. Some regions develop because of the land, water, weather, crops, or other features in the area. Some regions are small neighborhoods, while others are huge areas of land. Regions help people identify and describe places that are similar, even though they have differences, too.

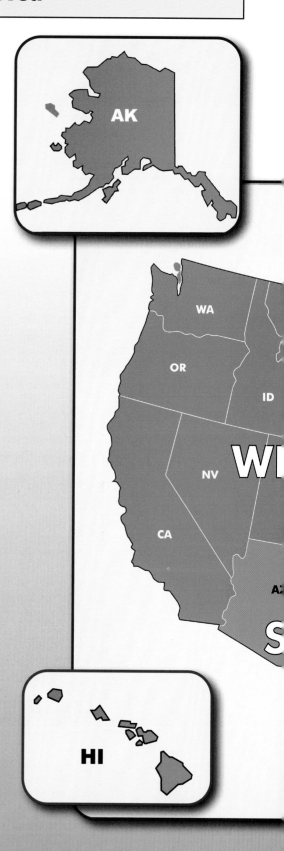

FIVE REGIONS

Different people divide the United States in different ways. In this series, the country is divided into five main regions. The regions are named for their locations on the map. They are the Northeast, the Southeast, the Midwest, the West, and the Southwest. Each region is made up of nearby states. In this book, you will discover some of the features that are shared by the states in a region.

America's Heartland

The Midwest is often called "America's Heartland" because it is in the heart, or central part, of the country. People who live in the Midwest region are called Midwesterners.

BY THE DOZEN

The Midwest region is made up of 12 states. The states can be divided into two groups—the Plains States and the Great Lakes States. The states in each group have similar land, weather, and other features.

The center of the United States is near Lebanon, Kansas. A small **monument** and American flag mark the spot.

THE PLAINS STATES

The Plains States are found in the western part of the Midwest. These states all have plains. Plains, or prairies, are huge areas of land that are mostly flat. Iowa, Kansas, Missouri, Nebraska, North Dakota, and South Dakota form this part of the Midwest.

Midwesterners are known as friendly, outgoing people who have a lot of "heart."

THE GREAT LAKES STATES

The Great Lakes States are found in the eastern part of the Midwest. Illinois, Indiana, Michigan, Minnesota, Ohio, and Wisconsin are in this group because they all border Great Lakes. The Great Lakes are a group of five lakes that make up the largest body of **fresh water** in the world. The states that border the Great Lakes are sometimes called the "Fresh Coast."

Shapes of the Midwest

There are many kinds of landforms in the Midwest. Landforms are the natural shapes of land on Earth. Plains, hills, mountains, caves, and bodies of water are all landforms.

The Sun sets on the golden plains of the Midwest.

FLAT LAND

The land in the Midwest is mostly flat. It was formed thousands of years ago when glaciers covered the region. Glaciers are enormous rivers of ice that form on mountains. When the glaciers melted, they spread across the Midwest, flattening hills and filling in valleys.

HILLS AND MOUNTAINS

Not all of the Midwest is flat, however. There are rolling hills in some areas. There are also the Black Hills. The Black Hills are a small mountain range, or group of mountains, in western South Dakota. There are many caves and **canyons** in the Black Hills.

Jewel Cave

Jewel Cave is located in the Black Hills region. It is the second-longest cave in the world. There are more than 150 miles (240 km) of passageways inside the cave!

THE BADLANDS

There are badlands in the western part of the Midwest. Badlands are dry, rocky areas of land that are shaped by wind and water over time. They have unusual rock formations, or shapes.

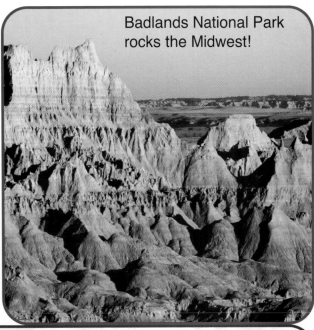
Badlands National Park rocks the Midwest!

The Black Hills rise high above the flat land of western South Dakota.

Midwest Waters

There are many lakes and rivers in the eastern part of the Midwest. The lakes were formed when glaciers carved deep holes in the land. The glaciers melted and the holes filled with water, becoming lakes. Some of the water spilled out of the lakes and formed rivers.

THE MIGHTY MISSISSIPPI

The Mississippi River runs through the middle of the Midwest region. It is the second-longest river in the United States. Many **tributaries** feed the Mississippi River. The Missouri, Ohio, and Illinois rivers all flow into the Mississippi, making it a wide and powerful river. The Mississippi has been an important shipping route for many years. People transport goods of all kinds on the "Mighty Mississippi."

An old-fashioned river boat chugs down the busy Mississippi River.

THE GREAT LAKES

Four of the Great Lakes are found in the Midwest region. They are Lake Superior, Lake Michigan, Lake Huron, and Lake Erie. The Great Lakes are great for the Midwest! The huge lakes give many people and animals fresh water to drink. They also provide water for crops. Rivers and **canals** join the Great Lakes to the Atlantic Ocean and Gulf of Mexico. The waterways allow big ships to travel into and out of the Great Lakes.

(right) This girl is skating through winter on a frozen lake in Minnesota.

(below) A huge ship on Lake Huron travels to the city of Detroit, Michigan.

LOTS OF LAKES

There are many smaller lakes and rivers in the Midwest, too. Many of those lakes are in Minnesota. It is called the "Land of 10,000 Lakes." In the summer, people use lakes throughout the Midwest for boating, fishing, and swimming. In the winter, Midwesterners skate and ice fish on frozen lakes and ponds.

Changing Weather

The climate of the Midwest changes from season to season and place to place. Climate is the type of weather that a region normally gets.

HOT AND COLD

In most parts of the Midwest, summers are warm and humid, or muggy. In the western part of the region, however, they can be very hot and dry. Winters are usually harsh throughout the Midwest. They bring freezing temperatures, biting winds, and a lot of snow to the region.

THE LAKE EFFECT

The Great Lakes bring extra snow to some nearby towns and cities. Wind carries moisture, or water, from the lakes. In winter, the water freezes and falls as snow. Parts of Ohio, Indiana, and Michigan all get very heavy "lake effect" snow. The Great Lakes also bring cool breezes to nearby places. Chicago, Illinois is called the "Windy City." Winds from Lake Michigan blow into Chicago and whistle through its busy streets.

These Midwesterners are digging out of a big winter snowstorm.

TORNADO ALLEY

There are many tornadoes in the Midwest plains each year. Tornadoes are violent storms with strong, whirling winds. They cause a lot of damage and hurt many people. Kansas has more tornadoes than any other state in the Midwest. It is part of Tornado Alley. Tornado Alley is an area in the United States where many tornadoes occur. Parts of Nebraska, South Dakota, Iowa, Wisconsin, and Minnesota are also in Tornado Alley.

Not in Kansas anymore

In *The Wizard of Oz* book and movie, a violent tornado strikes Kansas. It carries a girl named Dorothy—and her little dog, Toto—to a magical world called Oz.

A swirling tornado plows through a field in the Midwest.

A powerful tornado causes severe damage to a school in Greensburg, Kansas.

The First Peoples of the Midwest

Native Americans have lived in the Midwest for thousands of years. Different nations lived in different parts of the region and used the resources that were available to them.

WOODLANDS NATIONS

The Potawatomi, Kickapoo, Ho-Chunk, and many other nations lived in the wooded Great Lakes area. They were called Woodlands nations. Woodlands nations fished in the lakes and rivers, hunted and gathered food, and grew corn and other crops. They built homes using wooden frames and tree bark.

(left) Some Woodlands nations carved canoes out of logs and traveled on the region's lakes and rivers.
(bottom) Many Native nations built summer camps in the Great Lakes area.

PLAINS NATIONS

Plains nations lived on the flat, grassy plains of the Midwest. Some nations, such as the Cheyenne, traveled from place to place hunting herds of buffalo. They ate the meat of the buffalo and used their hides to make lightweight tents called tipis. Other nations, such as the Pawnee and Arikara, hunted buffalo but lived in villages. They built homes called earth lodges and grew crops to eat. Earth lodges are dome-shaped homes made of mud and grass.

EUROPEAN SETTLERS

In the 1500s, Spanish explorers brought horses to the United States. Native peoples used the horses to hunt and travel across the land. Soon, other Europeans began to explore the Midwest. Native peoples traded furs and hides with them for needles, fishhooks, tools, and other metal items. Britain and France began to **settle** in the Midwest. The countries fought one another to control the land.

(left) Some Native families lived in tipis that they could take apart and carry on the plains. (top) Native nations traded with Europeans to get goods they needed. (bottom) Other Plains nations lived in villages made up of many earth lodges.

Little Houses on the Prairies

The United States acquired the Midwest over time. In 1783, Americans took control of the Northwest Territory from Britain. Twenty years later, the United States purchased a huge area of land from France. The deal was known as the Louisiana Purchase. It gave the United States the rest of the Midwest region.

Sacagawea guided Lewis and Clark in their long journey through the Midwest.

EXPLORING THE MIDWEST

Americans began exploring their new land. Meriwether Lewis and William Clark traveled throughout the Midwest and beyond. They studied the area and made maps so it could be settled. A Native American woman named Sacagawea helped them travel and learn about the land.

SETTLING THE MIDWEST

In 1862, the United States government began giving away land west of the Mississippi River. To earn the land, however, people had to settle it and stay for at least five years. Many **pioneers** moved to the Midwest, where the soil was good for farming. They built homes and grew crops. Life was hard for the pioneers. It was also hard for Native Americans, who were forced from their lands.

GATEWAY TO THE WEST

Millions of settlers passed through St. Louis, Missouri, on their journey west. The city was a busy **trading post** near the middle of the Mississippi River. Today, a huge arch in St. Louis honors the city and the pioneers who traveled through it. The Gateway Arch is the highest monument in the country.

Wild about Wilder

Laura Ingalls Wilder wrote a series of books about pioneer life in the Midwest. The books—including *Little House in the Big Woods* and *Little House on the Prairie*—were first sold in the 1930s and are still popular today.

The Gateway Arch is made of stainless steel and stands 630 feet (190 m) high.

Town and Country

Today, nearly 67 million people live in the Midwest. Most Midwesterners live in cities near the region's lakes and rivers. Others live in small towns and farming communities throughout the region.

MISSISSIPPI MILLS

Many pioneers who were traveling west decided to settle along the Mississippi River. They cleared the land and built homes and farms. They floated crops and lumber down the river to mills. In gristmills, people ground grain into flour. In sawmills, they cut logs into boards.

BIG BUSINESS

In the early 1900s, people began building factories along the Mississippi River. They made steel, paper, and other products in the factories. They transported the products on the river and sold them around the world. Soon, places like St. Louis and Minneapolis grew into busy **manufacturing** centers. Many people left their farms to work in factories in the cities.

Midwesterners work in factories to manufacture goods that people need.

GREAT CITIES

Many people also settled near the Great Lakes. The cool water, thick forests, and rich farmland brought people to the region. Today, there are many busy cities in this part of the Midwest. Chicago is the third-largest city by population in the region. It is also the third-largest city in the United States. Detroit, Milwaukee, and Cleveland are other big cities on the shores of the Great Lakes.

(right) This Midwest farmer is up to his ears in corn!
(bottom) Cheers to Milwaukee! Located on the shores of Lake Michigan, it is the largest city in Wisconsin and is famous for brewing beer.

GROWING THE MIDWEST

Many families in the Midwest also live and work on farms. Farmers settled the region because it is good for growing crops. The land is mostly flat, there are many lakes and rivers to water plants, summers are warm, and the soil is rich in **nutrients**.

Natural Resources

The Midwest is rich in natural resources. A natural resource is something found in nature that people can use. Midwesterners depend on the water, soil, trees, and **minerals** in their region.

PLENTY OF WATER

The Midwest has many bodies of fresh water. Water is an important resource because it allows people to drink and catch fish to eat. It lets farmers water their crops.

Water also allows people to travel and carry goods from place to place.

TOPS FOR CROPS

The soil in the Midwest is very fertile, or good for growing crops. Farmers in the Midwest harvest many types of grains. They also grow soybeans, oilseeds, hay, fruits, and vegetables. They raise hogs, beef and dairy cows, and other farm animals.

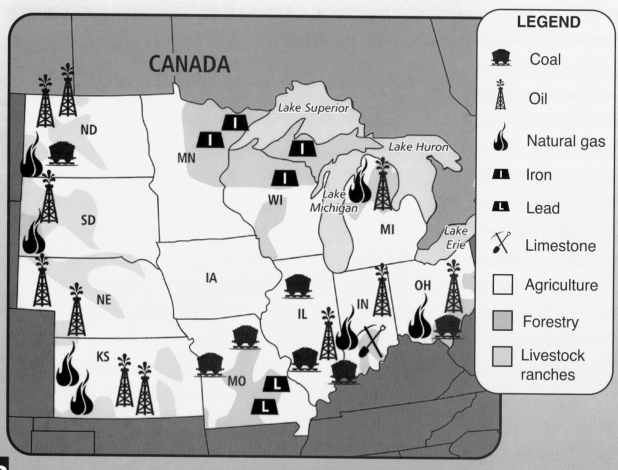

THICK FORESTS

There are thick forests in the northern parts of Minnesota, Wisconsin, and Michigan. Trees are a valuable resource because they provide lumber and paper. People use lumber to build homes, furniture, and other wood products.

(top) Tall trees grow in this Minnesota forest.
(below) Midwesterners mine limestone in this quarry.

MINING MINERALS

There are also many minerals in the Midwest. Minnesota produces most of the country's iron ore, while Missouri makes most of its lead. Miners get coal, oil, natural gas, limestone, and other important minerals from the ground in the Midwest. People use the minerals to make products they need and to heat their homes.

Say cheese!

Wisconsin is known as "America's Dairyland." It produces more cheese than any other state. In fact, it makes about a quarter of the country's cheese! Dairy farmers in Wisconsin also produce a lot of milk.

The Nation's Breadbasket

The Midwest is called "America's breadbasket." A breadbasket is the area of a country that produces most of its grain products. Farmers in the Midwest grow corn, wheat, oats, barley, sorghum, and other grains. They harvest the grains and store them in large bins. The bins are called grain elevators.

WHAT'S THE USE?

People use the grains to make breads, cereals, pasta, cakes, and many other foods. Farmers also use the grains to feed livestock, or farm animals. Although most corn grown in the Midwest is used to feed livestock, it has many other uses, too. People use corn to make cooking oil, sweeteners, starch, popcorn, and even fuel!

Way to grow, Kansas!

Kansas is known as "The Wheat State." It produces more wheat than any other state. In fact, farmers in Kansas grow about 400 million bushels of wheat each year!

THE CORN BELT

The Corn Belt is a region in the Midwest that produces a lot of corn. The region includes Iowa, Illinois, Nebraska, and Minnesota.

Together, these four states produce more than half the corn grown in the country! Iowa produces the most corn of all. It is sometimes called the "Tall Corn State."

These grain elevators in Iowa are overflowing with corn.

Farmers use big machines to harvest crops in the Midwest.

Making Money in the Midwest

The economy of the Midwest is based on the natural land resources and many waterways in the region. The economy of a place is how it produces and uses goods to make money.

MANUFACTURING

There are many factories in the Midwest. People build factories there because it has the natural resources they need to manufacture their products. Factories in the Midwest produce food, farm equipment, paper, furniture, computers, airplanes, cars, and many other products. Detroit, Michigan, is a busy manufacturing city. It is called the "Motor City" because factory workers build many cars there.

TRANSPORTATION

People also build factories in the Midwest because it is easy to transport goods there. Many factories in the region are located near rivers, lakes, and other waterways. People use the waterways to bring **raw materials** to the factories. They use the same waterways to ship the finished products to stores. Chicago, Indianapolis, and Kansas City are major transportation **hubs** in the Midwest.

This ship is delivering coal to a factory in the Motor City.

AGRICULTURE

Agriculture, or farming, is also very important to the economy of the Midwest. Farmers grow many types of fresh foods for people in the United States to eat. They also export many foods. To export is to send goods to another country in order to sell them.

TOURISM

Tourism is another important part of the economy in the Midwest. Tourism is traveling or visiting a place to have fun. Millions of people visit the region each year. Many come to see lively cities and interesting places. Others come for the region's lush land and refreshing lakes and rivers. See pages 28-29 for some famous Midwest sights.

(left) These trucks are filled to the brim with fresh grains to export.

The world's longest annual freshwater sailing race attracts tourists to Chicago's Navy Pier.

Midwest Mix

The Midwest is a mix of people and cultures. Culture is how groups of people express themselves through their art, music, food, and traditions.

RURAL AREAS

In the small towns and quiet farming communities of the Midwest, people lead **rural** lifestyles. They live on family farms and work hard in the fields. They grow food and use it to prepare simple, hearty meals. Homemade pies and breads, pot roasts, and stews are favorite foods. People gather at local fairs to show their best animals and have fun.

True North

North Dakota is the most rural state in the country. Almost all the land in North Dakota is used for farming. It is also considered one of the safest and friendliest states. In fact, "Dakota" is a Sioux word that means "**allies**."

A young Midwesterner proudly shows off her prize-winning steer at a rural fair.

EUROPEAN IMMIGRANTS

In the past, **immigrants** came to the Midwest to work on farms and in factories. They came from Germany, Ireland, Sweden, and other European countries. Their traditional foods—such as German sausages and Swedish pancakes—are popular throughout the region today. Their cultures are celebrated in festivals each year.

URBAN CENTERS

In the 1800s, many African Americans came to the Midwest. They fled to **free states** in the region to escape slavery in the southern United States. More African Americans later moved to Midwest cities to find work in factories. Today, Detroit, Cleveland, St. Louis, and many other Midwest cities have large African American populations. People from around the world move to these exciting **urban** centers. They proudly share their food, music, and traditions with other Midwesterners.

(left) German sausages and sauerkraut are popular foods in the Midwest.

People from around the world celebrate their cultures at festivals held in the region.

Discover the Midwest

The Midwest is known for its big crops, big lakes, and big smiles. There are plenty of big sights to see and many ways to have big fun in the middle of the country. Explore the region and discover why bigger is better in the Midwest!

BIG HEADS

Nearly three million tourists head to South Dakota each year to see the big faces on a mountain face. Mount Rushmore National Memorial is a huge sculpture carved into a mountain in the Black Hills region. The sculpture shows the heads of four larger-than-life American presidents—George Washington, Thomas Jefferson, Theodore Roosevelt, and Abraham Lincoln.

BIG SPLASH

The Wisconsin Dells has been a popular tourist attraction for more than 150 years. Early visitors came to see the Dells, or small valleys, and the unusual rock formations along the Wisconsin River. Today, tourists flock to the nearby city for its many water parks and family activities. About five million people visit the Dells each year.

Tourists get a big kick out of the big faces on Mount Rushmore.

BIG GAMES

There are big games—and big fans—in the Midwest! People from around the country gather in places like Green Bay, Detroit, Cincinnati, Milwaukee, and Chicago to cheer for their favorite sports teams. Baseball and football are big throughout the Midwest, and ice hockey is popular in the northern states.

BIG RACE

Fans race to Speedway, Indianapolis, to watch one of the biggest motorsports events in the world. The Indianapolis 500 is a 500-mile (800 km) car race held there each spring. Drivers reach high speeds and winners collect big prizes at the Indy 500.

BIG MALL

The Mall of America in Bloomington, Minnesota, is the biggest shopping center in the United States. The mall features a theme park, an aquarium, 14 movie theaters, and more than 520 stores! Forty million shoppers visit the mega-mall each year.

BIG CITY

Chicago is a big city with many big **skyscrapers**. The tallest building in the city is the Willis Tower (formerly the Sears Tower). It is the tallest building in the United States. Visitors can see Navy Pier, Lincoln Park, Wrigley Field, and other famous Chicago sights from the big tower. On a clear day, they can even see four other states in the Midwest!

Racing fans find fast cars and big thrills at the Indianapolis 500.

Timeline

1783 – The United States acquires the Northwest Territory from Britain. The area includes present-day Ohio, Indiana, Illinois, Michigan, Wisconsin, and part of Minnesota.

1803 – The United States buys a large area of land from France in the Louisiana Purchase. The area includes present-day Missouri, Iowa, Kansas, Nebraska, most of North Dakota and South Dakota, and part of Minnesota.

1804 – Meriwether Lewis and William Clark begin exploring the Midwest. They make maps and take notes about the land, plants, and animals in the region.

1825 – The Erie Canal opens. It connects the Great Lakes to the Atlantic Ocean for the first time.

1837 – John Deere invents the steel plow in Illinois. The strong farming tool allows people to prepare the soil in the Midwest for growing crops.

1860 – The Pony Express begins. It is a fast mail service with horseback riders based in St. Joseph, Missouri.

1862 – The United States government passes the Homestead Act. The law gives free land to pioneers who settle west of the Mississippi River.

1869 – The Transcontinental Railroad is completed. It allows people to travel quickly and safely through the Midwest.

1871 – The Great Chicago Fire destroys much of the city and kills hundreds of people.

1887 – Susanna M. Salter is elected mayor of Argonia, Kansas. She is the first woman to hold any political office in the United States.

1925 – The Tri-State Tornado hits Missouri, Illinois, and Indiana. It kills 695 people, making it the deadliest tornado in the history of the United States.

1927 – Gutzon Borglum begins carving Mount Rushmore National Memorial near Keystone, South Dakota. The project involves nearly 400 workers and takes 14 years to complete.

1967 – Two Midwest football teams face off in the first Super Bowl championship game ever played. The Green Bay Packers defeat the Kansas City Chiefs 35 to 10.

1973 – The Sears Tower is built in Chicago. At the time, it is the tallest building in the world. In 2009, it is renamed the Willis Tower.

1993 – Heavy snow and rain cause the Mississippi and Missouri rivers to overflow. The "Great Flood of 1993" kills many people and destroys 100,000 homes in the Midwest.

1997 – Barack Obama is elected to the Illinois Senate. In 2005, he serves as a U.S. Senator from Illinois. Four years later, Obama becomes the first African American President of the United States.

2011 – A large and violent series of tornadoes hits the United States in April. The storm—known as the 2011 Super Outbreak—lasts for more than three days. It brings high winds, severe thunderstorms, heavy rain, and flooding to the Midwest.

Find Out More

BOOKS

Curry, Elizabeth and Judson Curry. *Regions of the United States: The Midwest*. Heinemann-Raintree, 2007.

Doak, Robin. *How Geography Affects the United States: The Midwest*. Greenwood, 2002.

Purcell, Martha Sias. *Reading Essentials in Social Studies: The Midwest*. Perfection Learning, 2005.

Wilder, Laura Ingalls. *Little House on the Prairie 75th Anniversary Edition.* HarperCollins, 2010.

WEBSITES

Great Lakes Information Network: Teach Great Lakes: www.great-lakes.net/teach

Houghton Mifflin Social Studies: States and Regions: www.eduplace.com/ss/socsci/tx/books/bkd/ilessons/

Macmillan/McGraw-Hill: Our Country and Its Regions www.macmillanmh.com/socialstudies/2009/ss/student/ grade4/g4_index.html

University of Missouri eThemes: Midwest Region of the United States: http://ethemes.missouri.edu/themes/915?locale=en

Glossary

ally A person who joins another to achieve a common goal

border To be beside another country or area

canal A waterway built by people for shipping or traveling

canyon A deep, narrow valley with steep, high sides

free state A state in the United States that did not allow slavery

fresh water Water that does not contain a lot of salt and is safe to drink

hub A center of activity or heavy traffic

immigrant Someone who comes to a new country to live

manufacture To use machines to make goods to sell

mineral A solid chemical substance found in the ground

monument A structure built to honor or remember someone or something

nutrient A natural substance that helps plants and animals grow

pioneer Someone who moves to a new area where few people live

raw material A basic substance that is used to make a product

rural Having to do with farming or the country

settle To make a home and live in an area where few people live

skyscraper A very tall building in a city

state A part of a country with its own people, leaders, and rules

trading post A place where people meet and exchange goods

tributary A smaller river that flows into a larger river

urban Having to do with a town or city

Index